The Waco Siege

An American Tragedy

by

Jack Rosewood

&

Dwayne Walker

Copyright © 2015 by Wiq Media

ALL RIGHTS RESERVED

No part of this book may be reproduced, stored in a retrieval system, or transmitted in any form or by any means, electronic, mechanical, photocopying, recording, scanning, or otherwise, without the prior written permission of the publisher.

ISBN-13: 978-1523233526

Contents

INTRODUCTION 1

CHAPTER 1: The American West, Guns, and Religion 4

    God, Guns, and the West 6

    The Seventh Day Adventist Church 9

    The Emergence of the Branch Davidians 10

    Vernon Howell Leads a New Generation 12

    Howell's Raid on Mount Carmel 13

CHAPTER 2: From Vernon Howell to David Koresh 16

    Early Life 16

    The Making of a Prophet 18

    David Koresh 20

    The Seven Seals 22

    Polygamy and Other Moral Issues at Mount Carmel 25

CHAPTER 3: The Sinful Messiah 27

A Villain Made for the Media 27

The "Sinful Messiah" Series 28

Sex and Violence at Mount Carmel? 29

The Other Side of "Sinful Messiah" 31

CHAPTER 4: The ATF's Case against the Branch Davidians 34

A Lesser Known Federal Agency 34

The Case Opens 35

A Weak Case 37

CHAPTER 5: February 28, 1993 41

Operation Trojan Horse/Showtime 41

The Gun Battle 42

Death from Above? 44

The Botched Rooftop Entry 47

The Ceasefire 48

CHAPTER 6: The Siege 51

The FBI Takes Over 51

Signs of Hope? 53

The FBI Attempts to End the Siege 54

The Posse Comitatus Act 56

The FBI Works against Itself 58

CHAPTER 7: Outside Support for the Davidians **60**

Constitutionalists and Right Wing Populists 60

Local Community Members 61

Other Branch Davidian Supporters 64

CHAPTER 8: April 19, 1993 .... **68**

Jumping the Gun? 68

The Final Assault Begins 70

The Fire 72

More Evidence for CS Gas as the Cause of the Fire 74

Immediate Results of the April 19 Raid 76

CHAPTER 9: The Aftermath **79**

The Criminal Trial of the Branch Davidians 79

Congressional Hearings 85

The Rise of the Militia Movement 87

Some Last Notes on Those Involved with the Waco Siege .. 91

Conclusion **93**

A Note From The Author **96**

Bibliography...97

Introduction

To many Americans thirty five years and older, the word "Waco" invokes strong images and opinions that are sometimes polarizing and almost always emotional. "Waco" has become a by-word, a euphemism, for an out of control government that seeks to oppress and kill its own people for some, while for others it has come to be associated with the danger of cults and religious extremism.

From February 28 until April 19, 1993, Americans were anxiously fixed to their television sets watching to see how the standoff between David Koresh and his followers, often referred to as the "Branch Davidians," and the government would end in a rural area a few miles outside of Waco, Texas. Since the standoff began violently, most thought it would end violently, but few were ready for the level of carnage that appeared on their television screens.

On April 19 the United States government, led by the Federal Bureau of Investigation (FBI), attacked the Branch Davidian's complex, known as Mount Carmel, with military tanks and CS gas that ended in a fire of biblical proportions that killed seventy six Davidians, which included nineteen children ages fifteen and younger and two fetuses.

The images of Mount Carmel burning shocked, saddened, and angered Americans from Maine to California and from Minnesota to Florida. "How could our government do such a thing?" was a common question; but equally puzzling to many was the enigmatic religious sect that called Mount Carmel its home and the even more mysterious leader who seemed to exercise an incredible, perhaps even deadly, hold over the Davidians.

The events that took place in those fifty one days in 1993 left repercussions that continue to affect American culture to this day. Anger over the government's handling of the Mount Carmel raid(s) provided the impetus for the exponential growth of the American militia movement and contributed directly to the bombing of the federal building in Oklahoma City, Oklahoma by militant, Timothy McVeigh.

Beyond the paramilitary training camps in rural America that the militias used to train their members, many average Americans began to question if the government really had their best interests in mind. Truly, today many thirty and forty something Americans – Generation X – point to the Waco Siege as a defining moment in their childhoods and young adulthoods, where they first came to the realization that life is not always fair and that as good as the United States is, it also has some obvious inherent problems.

After the Waco Siege, the issues of religious freedom and gun ownership – two bedrocks of American culture that are codified in the United States Constitution – also entered mainstream political debates. People asked questions such as the following: how many guns should people be allowed to own and how much freedom should be given to "non-mainstream" religious groups?

Although the Waco Siege only lasted fifty one days, the story of how it happened and the ramifications it had on American society is quite complex. Waco was a true American tragedy; one that clearly could have been avoided, but also one where people on both sides aggravated the situation. In that respect the story of the Waco Siege is a cautionary tale because, unfortunately, it could happen again.

CHAPTER 1:
The American West, Guns, and Religion

In order to understand how and why the Waco Siege took place and possibly how it could have been avoided, a brief examination of how the Branch Davidians fit into the unique culture and history of the American West is warranted. The role that the United States Constitution, or at least interpretations of it, played in the Davidians' ideology must also be considered.

When the United States Congress ratified its new nation's constitution in 1787 it differed little from those of other Western European nations of the time; it outlined the form of the government and how powers would be delegated by the different branches. What set the United States Constitution apart from those of Europe was the inclusion of the Bill of Rights – ten amendments that essentially limit the central government's power – in 1791.

The First Amendment and therefore the most important to the Constitution's framers, concerns ideas of freedom of speech, religion, and assembly. The text reads: "Congress shall make no law respecting an establishment of religion, or prohibiting the free exercise thereof; or abridging the freedom of speech, or of the press; or the right of the people peaceably to assemble, and to petition the Government for a redress of grievances."

The limits of the amendment have been challenged in the courts on numerous occasions and certain legal precedents have been established: it has been deemed illegal to advocate crime such as rebellion or murder, but "hate speech" is protected under the amendment. Lies and libelous speech are also not protected, with offenders being potential subject to lawsuits but not criminal prosecution. In terms of the Waco Siege, the first clause of the First Amendment and the one pertaining to peaceful assembly are the pertinent points.

Equally important to the First Amendment in understanding the Waco Siege is the Second Amendment. The text of the Second Amendment reads: "A well regulated militia being necessary to the security of a free state, the right of the people to keep and bear arms shall not be infringed."

The Second Amendment has experienced a more contentious history and has been challenged many more times in the courts, but the core of the text, the second clause, has never been threatened in American history. Most of the limits imposed on the Second Amendment by Congress throughout American history have been concentrated on how many guns individuals should be allowed to own and what type of guns. For instance, should Americans be allowed to collect arsenals comprised of hundreds of military grade weapons? The initial raid on Mount Carmel concerned both of these points and is therefore extremely important when considering the context of the Waco Siege.

But the Branch Davidians were neither the first obscure religious sect in American history, nor the first to amass a considerable arsenal of guns; in many ways they were just carrying on a long tradition that has been common in the American West.

God, Guns, and the West

Since the nineteenth century the American West has drawn a plethora of different people to its mountains and prairies who felt restricted by the urban sprawl west of the Mississippi. A diverse batch of religious zealots, pioneers, reformers, outlaws, and lawmen made the western territories and later states, their homes and helped inspire the imagination of people around the world. During the middle of the twentieth century, dime store novels written by authors such as Zane Grey and Louis L'Amour and television shows like *The Rifleman* and *Gunsmoke* captured the spirit of the American West in fiction; but often fiction was not far from reality.

Pioneers who came to the newly opened western territories in the nineteenth century often had to rely on themselves and their neighbors for protection from hostile Indians and outlaws. Frontier pioneers also had to be their own doctors, which helped to further the independent nature of these people. Most ranches and farmsteads had several guns and when malfeasants were captured, justice was usually swift and sharp.

By the middle of the nineteenth century a culture developed in the American West that is still apparent there today: somewhat socially conservative, yet Libertarian, western states were among the first in the United States to give women the right to vote. Westerners loved their god and guns, but did not like to tell others how to live their lives and did not like the government telling them how to live theirs. Among the many different sects that made the American West their home in the nineteenth century, the group with the most similarities to the Branch Davidians was the Mormons.

The Mormons – officially known as the Church of Jesus Christ of Latter-day Saints – began as an obscure Christian sect in the region of upstate New York known as the "burned over district" in 1830. The region earned its moniker because of the numerous religious revivals that were taking place there in the early nineteenth century and the plethora of new sects that formed in the locale. Joseph Smith was just one of many prophets in the region, but his revelation was unique – god had revealed to him a new set of books to the Bible, which became known as the Book of Mormon.

Smith collected a sizable following, but also immense hostility from the locals so he led his followers to Ohio and then Nauvoo, Illinois where they established a colony. Resentment by local residents and authorities over the Mormons' practice of polygamy led to Smith's assassination in 1844 and the sacking of their town in 1846. In 1847 Brigham Young, who became the Mormon leader after Smith's murder, led his followers out west to what would later became the state of Utah. Distrust of the government led to numerous conflicts between the Mormons and federal authorities, most notably in the bloodless rebellion known as the Utah War of 1857.

Although the Branch Davidians were not Mormons, they shared some common threads in their histories, most notably the practice of polygamy and a distrust of the federal government. The theological origins of the Branch Davidians though can be traced directly to another sect that also traces its origins to the burned over district – the Seventh Day Adventists

The Seventh Day Adventist Church

Around the same time that Joseph Smith and his followers were being persecuted in Illinois, a new Christian theology was being formulated in upstate New York. In the 1840s, a nondescript man named William Miller began to preach that the end of the world was near. Eschatological, or end times, theology was nothing new to Christianity in the mid-nineteenth century, especially in Protestantism, but Miller's ideas were new in that he predicted a specific date for the end – October 22, 1844. When the date arrived Miller and a number of his followers were waiting in a rural area of upstate New York for the end, or the "Advent" as he termed it, to come, which of course it never did. Disheartened, many of Miller's followers denounced him as a fraud and returned to their old churches, but some went on to expand on his vision.

One person who was particularly drawn to Miller's vision was a woman named Ellen G. White. White argued that Miller was essentially correct, but that his math was incorrect and that the Advent that the prophet preached about was still to come. Besides affirming the eschatological vision of Miller, White also proposed new practices to go along with the end times theology such as keeping the Sabbath from sundown Friday until sundown Sunday, which coincides with that of the Judaism instead of other Christian faiths that recognize Sunday as the day of the Sabbath. Truly, the new church took a decidedly Old Testament stance on many ritualistic and theological issues in addition to the Sabbath; followers were to keep a diet that conformed to the Old Testament book of Leviticus, which meant they were to eschew such foods as pork and shrimp. Miller also imbued her followers – officially formed as the General Conference of Seventh-Day Adventists in 1863 – with other ideas not found directly in the bible.

White preached a proto-feminist theology that held that not only should women be allowed to play a prominent role in the Church, but also that the Holy Spirit was essentially a feminine aspect of god. Also, White added a certain amount of anti-government ideology into the Seventh Day Adventist Church.

For decades the Seventh Day Adventist Church grew, not just in the United States, but eventually members proselytized throughout the world, gaining new followers on almost every continent. It would be a non-American convert to the Church who led a break from the main body that ultimately formed the Branch Davidian sect.

The Emergence of the Branch Davidians

In 1918, a Bulgarian immigrant named Victor Houteff made a decision that not only changed his life, but would change the lives of many others and continued to affect the lives of scores of people for nearly 100 years later – he converted to the Seventh Day Adventist Church. Houteff's conversion was nothing extraordinary in itself, but a zealous belief in the Church combined with his somewhat dubious and inauspicious background not only make for an interesting story, but go a long way in explaining some of the attitudes that David Koresh and the Branch Davidians held during the fifty one day standoff in 1993.

The details on Houteff's immigration to the United States are murkey, but through hard work he was able to establish himself as a member in good standing of both the Seventh Day Adventist community and in the Los Angeles area where he resided throughout the 1920s. Houteff showed an aptitude for scriptural knowledge despite only having a third grade education and English being his second language. Eventually, Houteff tired of the main body SDA Church as he felt they had grown too permissive, so he took some followers to the plains outside Waco, Texas in 1933.

Houteff promised his followers that Waco would be a promised land and so to impress this idea on his acolytes he christened their new colony "Mount Carmel." In the Old Testament book, I Kings, Mount Carmel is the location where the Israelite prophet Elijah killed the followers of the Phoenician god Baal. The militancy of the name of the new home of Houteff and his followers perhaps foreshadowed the events that took place there fifty years later.

After the establishment of Mount Carmel, Houteff made the split from the main body SDA Church official when he renamed the Mount Carmel sect the "Davidian Seventh-Day Adventist Church" in 1942.

Houteff's sect prospered and was stable for many years until he died in 1955, which then resulted in an interregnum until Benjamin Roden assumed the mantle of leadership in 1959. Theologically speaking, Roden followed most of his successor's ideas, but gradually moved the sect in a more Old Testament-centric, neo-Hebrew direction. The sect also became known as the "Branch" at this time by the main body of the SDA Church, although Davidians who were part of the 1993 siege claim that they never referred to themselves as such.

Vernon Howell Leads a New Generation

After Benjamin Roden died in 1978, the Branch Davidians experienced a power vacuum and turmoil that was not apparent when Houteff passed. George Roden, Benjamin's son, believed that either he or his elderly mother Lois should lead the Davidians, but a twenty year old upstart named Vernon Howell had other ideas.

Vernon Howell, who the world now knows as David Koresh, was a bit of a rebel among the conservative Branch Davidians and in many ways represented the younger generation of Seventh Day Adventists. Howell wore t-shirts, jeans, and often kept his hair longer, which angered the more conservative Branch Davidians who were led by George Roden. Roden may have been further angered by Howell's claims that he was involved sexually with Lois, who was forty years his senior. Eventually, Howell left with a group of followers to Palestine, Texas, but before he did he married fourteen year old Rachel Jones, which was legal in Texas at the time if done with parental consent. While in Palestine, a war of words developed between Howell and Roden that eventually ended in a shootout.

Howell's Raid on Mount Carmel

History can be a funny thing sometimes. Major events are often the result of one or two events, which may be true in the case of the Waco Siege. While Howell and his new group of followers were living in Palestine, Roden appeared to be more concerned with proving that the former was a false prophet instead of developing his own theology or proselytizing to the masses. Perhaps he was angry that most of the community followed Howell to Palestine, or maybe he resented the possible relationship that his mother had with the young prophet, but eventually his rivalry with Howell bordered on obsession.

In 1987 Roden came up with an idea that he believed would lift the veil of piousness off of Howell and show his followers that he was a fraud. Perhaps Roden was spending too much time alone at the Mount Carmel community because none of his followers told him that not only was his plan bizarre, but also ill-conceived and quite juvenile. He dug up the remains of a Branch Davidian named Anna Hughes who was buried at Mount Carmel and challenged Howell to raise her from the dead.

Perhaps in Roden's twisted world he thought that Howell was equally twisted and would try to attempt the feat, but if so, then he severely misjudged Howell's intelligence and sanity.

Howell reacted to the morbid news by visiting the local police with a couple of other members. The police told Howell that if Roden did in fact disinter Hughes' body, then a crime has been committed, but proving said crime would be another matter. Local law enforcement said that they could do nothing about it unless he had some tangible proof, which there was no way for *them* to get without a search warrant.

As Howell and his followers left the police station they resolved to get the proof – any way possible!

On November 3, 1987 Howell and seven other Davidians went shopping at local hardware and sporting goods stores for the tools that they would need to get the goods on Roden: boots, camouflage fatigues, and bullets for their guns. Howell and the others were determined to take pictures of the disinterred corpse, but they all knew that Roden was well armed and would not hesitate to shoot any intruders, especially ones he considered apostates.

When the squad arrived at Mount Carmel they were quickly met with gunfire, which they promptly returned. As the firefight between the two Branch Davidian factions continued, eventually neighbors called the police who then arrived and took Howell and his followers into custody. The eight men were charged with attempted murder, but were acquitted of all counts in April. 1988.

After the providential verdict was announced, Howell and his followers quickly took control of Mount Carmel as Roden was in jail on contempt of court charges for six months. Howell and the Davidians paid the back taxes owed on Mount Carmel and legally secured their return, while Roden has spent most of his life in mental hospitals. With one simple, bizarre act Roden set into motion the events that would culminate with the tragic siege of Mount Carmel in 1993.

Vernon Howell's place as the leader of the Branch Davidians and the king of Mount Carmel was established and the leader also learned that sometimes violence does indeed pay!

CHAPTER 2:
From Vernon Howell to David Koresh

Early Life

The journey that Vernon Howell took from average working class Texan to the leader and prophet of an obscure religious sect was both arduous and circuitous, but not unlike that of many others in history who have risen to fame and/or infamy.

Vernon Howell was born in 1959 to Bobby Howell and fourteen year old Bonnie Clark. The circumstances of Howell's birth are somewhat ironic and foreshadowed elements in his adult life: he was born the same year Benjamin Roden took control of Mount Carmel and his mother was the same age as the girl he married.

Howell's childhood can best be described as tumultuous, although there are few sources to confirm any of the anecdotes that Koresh later gave to reporters and others about his childhood. His mother never married his father, so he was forced to live with stepfathers, who Howell claimed were physically abusive, and eventually his grandparents. Vernon's only sibling was a younger brother named Roger who would later compile an extensive rap sheet.

With little support at home it is no surprise that the young Howell performed poorly in school.

"I already failed the first grade twice, so I failed the second grade," said Howell about his problems in elementary school. Howell's early academic problems resulted in his being placed in remedial classes where he earned the nickname, "Mr. Retardo." Needless to say, the moniker and taking part in the remedial classes definitely hurt young Vernon's self-esteem as he recalled: "I mean you're, you know, 'here comes the retarded kids.' And it's like I stopped in my tracks."

Howell was a particularly poor speller, which points to dyslexia, a learning disability that was rarely diagnosed as such before the 1980s, but is routinely diagnosed and treated today.

Despite his early academic problems, Vernon Howell showed great aptitude in two areas – mechanics and theology. After Vernon received a new radio as a gift from his mother, the boy took the appliance apart to see how it functioned. As he got older, his love of mechanics coincided with a love of cars – the faster the better. Howell's mechanical side also brought him to a more artistic side when he found and fixed up an old guitar in an abandoned barn. He would carry his love of music until his final days and during his life used it to promote his theological beliefs, for which he showed the most aptitude.

Vernon Howell was raised in the strict confines of the Seventh Day Adventist Church, so while many other boys his age were chasing girls and/or experimenting with drugs and alcohol, he was working on his future craft. He constantly read the scriptures and devoured any biblical lectures and sermons he could find on television, magazines, and other various other printed tracts. His devotion to the Bible certainly alienated him from many young people his own age, but through it he was able to develop his own unique style that would later become synonymous with David Koresh.

The Making of a Prophet

In the late 1970s Howell became involved with the Mount Carmel Branch Davidian community and in 1981 he moved there fulltime. At this point in his life he learned that sermons about some of the more esoteric passages of the Bible attracted a number of followers who were eager to learn the word of God; but bringing in new followers was only half the battle – he needed to keep those people interested.

Howell's preaching style definitely caught the attention of his followers and anyone else who happened to hear one of his sermons. He often stood in front of his followers with shoulder length hair, wearing either jeans or sweat pants and usually a t-shirt instead of a button up. Howell's appearance certainly bucked the mainstream SDA establishment, which was conservative to say the least. But Vernon's message was not meant for the converted, he saw himself as a latter day messiah and like the first messiah, he would take his message to the masses.

Among the Branch Davidians who followed Howell to Palestine and then back to Mount Carmel were former drinkers, drug users, and womanizers. Howell did not discriminate when it came to proselytizing prospective followers on the basis of race, national origin, or background, however lurid it may be. Besides Howell's folksy appearance at the pulpit, he also presented his sermons in matter of fact ways much easier for the uninitiated to understand.

Howell was known for delivering his sermons in an emotional but conversational style and more importantly he loved to use metaphors that everyone could understand, no matter how offensive some may have found them. For instance, in one particular sermon Howell compared sin to boogers!

"That nasty old sin, how can you get rid of the stuff? It's like a booger on your fingers, right? You're trying, you know, and you're picking, and it gets on your other finger? Even when you're going 50 miles an hour down the road and you're trying to flick it off! I know what I'm talking about you see!" proclaimed Howell in front of his followers. And Howell did know what he was talking about as he claimed to be a sinner like anyone else, a blemished sacrificial goat in biblical parlance. Howell's preaching style, metaphors, and even his sins all resonated deeply with his followers. As Branch Davidian Livingston Fagan said, "When you criticized David for something he did, you were really only criticizing yourself."

Howell found his niche and a certain level of charisma that is needed to be such a leader. He was not a particularly imposing or attractive specimen – he was average height and looks – but his scriptural knowledge and preaching style captivated his followers and gave them a sense of purpose in life. As Howell's following grew and became more loyal, he took things to the next level.

David Koresh

Today, the name David Koresh evokes almost as many, if not more, feelings in people familiar with it than the word Waco. At first glance, the strangely exotic sounding name sounds like something an unstable person would choose on a whim, but Howell's choice of appellation was not capricious.

In the summer of 1990, Howell legally changed his name to David Koresh in what can be described as a process and ultimate affirmation of his theological beliefs. The first name, David, is obviously taken from the Old Testament King David who many today know as the boy that slew the Philistine giant

Goliath, but was also the second king of the earthly Kingdom of Israel. Throughout the books of Chronicles and Kings, David's prowess as a warrior against god's enemies are related numerous times as is his sexual virility. As will be detailed more below, Koresh believed that he carried both of those Davidic qualities within him.

Howell's new surname, Koresh, is perhaps the more exotic aspect of the name, but no less biblical. Koresh is the Hebrew version of the ancient Persian king Cyrus' name, who in 539 BC famously conquered Babylon and then allowed the captive Jews to return to Israel to rebuild the Solomonic Temple, as related in the Old Testament book of Ezra. The two names combined tell a lot about the prophet and preacher's vision, which he claims came to him on a trip to Israel in 1985.

In 1985 Howell and other Branch Davidians made a pilgrimage to the state of Israel to visit the holy sites mentioned in both the Old and New Testaments. Howell was actually unimpressed with the real Mount Carmel, but he claims that the true spiritual experience he had while in the holy land came when he was brought to the heavens on a celestial chariot. Once in the heavens, he claimed that much was revealed to him, but foremost were the secrets to the enigmatic "Seven Seals" of the book of Revelation.

The prophet now had his message to bring to the world.

The Seven Seals

In order to truly understand David Koresh, the Branch Davidians, and the Waco Siege, one must examine how the prophet of Mount Carmel interpreted the cryptic Seven Seals of Revelation. Many protestant sects view the book as a prophecy about the end times, while the Catholic Church's official view is that it is commentary. Most protestant biblical scholars believe that each seal represents a progression towards the apocalypse and the eventual return of Christ to the earth, but there is no consensus on what each seal represents.

The verses that detail the Seven Seals read in part:
And I wept much, because no man was found worthy to open and to read the book, neither to look thereon. And one of the elders saith unto me, Weep not: behold, the Lion of the tribe of Judah, the Root of David, hath prevailed to open the book, and to loose the seven seals thereof. And I beheld, and, lo, in the midst of the throne and of the four beasts, and in the midst of the elders, stood a Lamb as it had been slain, having seven horns and seven eyes, which are the seven Spirits of God sent forth into all the earth. (Rev. 5:4-6)

The verses can obviously be interpreted in several different ways, but any prophetic explanation is tinged with an apocalyptic vibe. Clearly, Koresh modelled the core of his theological message around these verses: only he could open, or interpret, the seals since he was the "root of David" and the Lamb of God on earth. Furthermore, the clause that describes the slain Lamb was eerily prophetic of Koresh's demise in 1993, or perhaps he made it a self-fulfilling prophecy.

What is known of Koresh's interpretations of the Seven Seals – he never published them, which was a point of contention between him and the FBI during the fifty one day standoff – is one where violence consumed the world. In particular, his translations of the Second and Fourth Seals are known through his surviving followers.

The text of the Second Seal reads:
And when he had opened the second seal, I heard the second beast say, Come and see. And there went out another horse that was red: and power was given to him that sat thereon to take peace from the earth, and that they should kill one another: and there was given unto him a great sword. (Rev. 6:3-4)

The violence prophesied in the Second Seal coincides with that of the Fourth Seal, which reads:
And when he had opened the fourth seal, I heard the voice of the fourth beast say, Come and see. And I looked, and behold a pale horse: and his name that sat on him was Death, and Hell followed with him. And power was given unto them over the fourth part of the earth, to kill with sword, and with hunger, and with death, and with the beasts of the earth. (Rev. 6:7-8)

The violence and apocalyptic prophecy of the book of Revelation is enough to make many good Christians cringe because it is difficult to reconcile those aspects of the Bible with the messages of peace and love that Jesus preached in the Gospels. But David Koresh was no ordinary Christian – he seemed to relish the violence of Revelation. "The Bible is a whole book about nothing but killing," Koresh once told his followers.

As Koresh offered his interpretation of the Seven Seals, he also began to make more grandiose claims. He stated that only the Lamb of God could interpret the Seals and that therefore he was the Lamb, a messiah; but Koresh never went so far as to claim to actually be God, or Jesus, instead merely a divine prophet in a long line of prophets. On this subject he said to his followers: "Now we may believe the message of Christ, 2,000 years ago, but of course, when it was being given, nobody believed it . . . When you have a dead prophet, you have a dead voice . . . You have someone that's not even here to get on your back and tell you you'd better shape up."

Koresh's followers believed that he was the living prophet, the Lamb, who would get them to shape up by revealing the Seven Seals.

Ultimately, Koresh's interpretation of the Seven Seals was what gave him legitimacy as a leader and prophet and allowed him to have a hold over his followers; his interpretation was like a key to some arcane and esoteric knowledge that allowed his followers to enter into heaven, albeit at a lower level than him.

Polygamy and Other Moral Issues at Mount Carmel

Koresh's interpretation of the Seven Seals was not the only theological tool he used to hold power over his followers; he culled several passages from the Bible, primarily the Old Testament, as examples of how the inhabitants at Mount Carmel should live. As the siege went on in 1993 and filtered reports of life inside Mount Carmel were made public, one aspect that shocked many was Koresh's practice of polygamy.

Koresh believed that as the prophet of the Branch Davidians and as the Lamb of God, he must father many children with different women. He based his idea on the book of Isaiah, but the Old Testament is full of a plethora of examples where Israelite and Hebrew kings, patriarchs, and prophets advocated plural marriage. Whether or not Koresh practiced polygamy for purely religious reasons is open to debate, but in the prophet's own words he equated the practice with a type of religious militancy as he said: "If you don't win in the bedroom, son, you're not going to win on the battlefield." By Koresh's standards he certainly won in the bedroom as he sired seventeen children, two with underage girls and others with adult women who were already married.

Just before Koresh officially changed his name, he proscribed celibacy for all male members of the Davidian sect at Mount Carmel, with the exception of him of course. By 1990 Koresh had effectively made Mount Carmel his own harem, complete with wives and concubines much as his namesakes David and Cyrus had done over 2,000 years before him.

Perhaps sensing sexual frustration among the male inhabitants of Mount Carmel, Koresh eased some traditional SDA restrictions. He lifted the ban on alcohol and tobacco use, although still frowned upon, was often ignored. Illicit drugs were still banned from the premises and despite the easing of rules, Mount Carmel never became a raucous party house. Members of the Branch Davidian band enjoyed a few beers while they jammed with their prophet and worked on new material, but that was the extent of drinking at Mount Carmel.

Ultimately, despite the non-mainstream rules of Mount Carmel that the inhabitants were to abide by, they were free to leave at any time and several did up until the complex was burned to the ground.

CHAPTER 3:
The Sinful Messiah

A Villain Made for the Media

During the Waco Siege in 1993, David Koresh was portrayed by most major media outlets in a negative light to say the least. "Charlatan," "freak," "deranged," "cult leader," and "the wacko in Waco" were just some of the adjectives that most average Americans used to describe the Branch Davidian leader; but their conclusions about Koresh and the rest of the Branch Davidians, was for the most part based on a decidedly one sided depiction. Reports that showed Koresh and the Branch Davidians in a more positive light did not emerge until after the tragic events of April 19, 1993 and even before the siege began on February 28, the local Waco media was busy painting the self-proclaimed prophet as a demented cult leader

In some ways Koresh played into the negative portrayal, but the media did more than its part in making him into a monster.

The "Sinful Messiah" Series

On February 27, the day before the Bureau of Alcohol, Tobacco, and Firearms (usually abbreviated with the acronym ATF) raid on Mount Carmel, the *Waco Tribune-Herald* released the first part of its seven part series titled, "Sinful Messiah" by Mark England and Darlene McCormick. The series proved to be a scathing report about Koresh and the Branch Davidians and ultimately set the tone for how larger media outlets reported on the situation as they used both writers as sources. A closer investigation of the series reveals that England and McCormick used questionable methods and often failed to demonstrate journalistic integrity.

Despite taking several months to compile, England and McCormick used a very limited amount of sources in their investigation. Besides consulting various members of law enforcement who were investigating the Branch Davidians, the two journalists used three disgruntled Branch Davidians, turned ATF informants, as their primary sources.

Among the three former Branch Davidians that England and McCormick interviewed was a young Australian man named Marc Breault. The young Australian found the Branch Davidians in the mid-1980s and then quickly moved to the United States to be near Koresh and the other Davidians. Breault claims he was happy in his new home and by all accounts Koresh and the other Davidians were happy with him, but things quickly changed in 1989.

As discussed above, Koresh (who still went by Vernon Howell at the time), proscribed celibacy for all male members in 1989 and shortly after began to take Branch Davidian women as his wives and concubines. Koresh chose Marc Breault's wife as his own, which infuriated the Australian who then quickly left the group. Although Breault's wife was far from Koresh's grasp in Australia, the event forever pushed the young man away from Koresh and eventually towards the ATF. Still being an ardent believer in the SDA theology in general and the Branch Davidian sect in particular, Breault attempted to start his own breakaway sect in 1990, but was ultimately not successful.

Sex and Violence at Mount Carmel?

Breault took his resentment towards Koresh first to the ATF, which concluded that he could offer them nothing substantial, and eventually to England and McCormick. Unlike the ATF, England and McCormick found high value in Breault's stories about the polygamy that was taking place at Mount Carmel.

Through interviews with Breault about life inside Mount Carmel, England and McCormick were able to paint a salacious picture of the Branch Davidians that was comprised of ample amounts of polygamy and sex with underage girls.

Despite his cooperation, Breault saw nothing wrong with either activity. On polygamy he pointed to several biblical verses that advocated the practice and numerous personalities, including King David, who were practitioners.

Perhaps the public could reconcile Koresh's practice of polygamy; it may have been strange and illegal, but most Americans would not care if it was between two consenting adults in the privacy of their own homes. But sex with underage girls was another matter. On this point, Breault pointed out that the girls were teenagers and nothing was done without the consent of their parents.

Essentially, Koresh's sexual activities with underage girls amounted to statutory rape, which although still a felony punishable by prison time, carries a far lesser sentence than pedophilia. Polygamy is also a crime in every American state, but rarely prosecuted by authorities.

Any good writer knows that there are certain elements that can be added to a story, must be added, in order to invoke a proper emotional response from readers. In the modern world and perhaps since the beginning of human civilization, the two elements that have consistently been employed to provoke the most emotion, thereby selling the most copies, are sex and violence.

The "Sinful Messiah" series certainly employed plenty of lurid tales about Koresh's sexual behaviors to entice readers, but a layer of violence, or perceived violence, was added to keep the masses reading. The report focused on the large arsenal of guns that were kept at Mount Carmel, which was the primary reason the Branch Davidians were being investigated by the ATF. England and McCormick formed the perfect link that could sell their series and make their careers.

The gun aspects of the reports focused on the high number of weapons stored at Mount Carmel and used plenty of loaded terms such as "assault weapons" and "machine guns". To most gun collectors, neither of those terms holds much meaning as a shotgun can be classified as an "assault weapon" if used against someone and the term "machine gun" is equally ambiguous.

The Other Side of "Sinful Messiah"

In the end, England and McCormick cannot be faulted for appealing to sensationalism in order to sell their series, but they can be blamed for failing to present a truly objective image of their subject. Journalists are humans so they are bound to have opinions concerning their stories, but throughout the "Sinful Messiah" series England and McCormick committed numerous errors that would have gotten a college journalism major a failing grade.

At its core, the "Sinful Messiah" series never presented life at Mount Carmel from the perspective of David Koresh or any of his loyal followers. As mentioned above, the few sources that were used were disgruntled former members and even then, only three were consulted. England and McCormick also never explained that there are biblical justifications for polygamy and failed to point out the difference between automatic and semi-automatic rifles, or that all of the guns they knew about at Mount Carmel were legal.

Surviving Branch Davidians have stated that they were most disturbed at how they were portrayed as a group: an angry cult of highly armed rednecks who shut themselves off from the outside world. The truth is that the Branch Davidians came from nearly every continent and many were of black, Hispanic, and Asian ethnicities. Also, firearm knowledge was not a requirement to live at Mount Carmel and in fact many members did not know how to shoot a gun. Many Branch Davidians were also quite educated and several held advanced degrees, which was not mentioned in the series, further adding to the perception that they were backwoods religious nuts. Also, Mount Carmel was not shut off from the outside.

Many Branch Davidians regularly visited Waco and some had jobs in town. Koresh particularly enjoyed checking out the local live music scene and was known to sit in with bands whose members he knew. At no time in Mount Carmel's history is there any evidence that any member was not allowed to leave the premises. In fact, during the fifty one day siege, many members left until and including the final tragic day of April 19. Over the several decades of Mount Carmel's existence, many children were raised there and several often left to work, attend college, or to start families. The children who left Mount Carmel were always welcome to return and many did, somewhat like Amish teens who are allowed to leave their communities until they decide they want to return as full members.

Despite being essentially a commune, the inhabitants of Mount Carmel were never required to give their possessions to the community or sign over their bank accounts and financial holdings to Koresh. The Branch Davidians of Mount Carmel followed a strict moral code, had a charismatic and by most accounts strange leader, and lived communally; but it would be difficult to define them as a "cult."

But that is exactly what the "Sinful Messiah" series did — branded the Branch Davidians as a cult who were blindly led by their charismatic, yet evil leader David Koresh.

CHAPTER 4:
The ATF's Case against the Branch Davidians

A Lesser Known Federal Agency

Lurid sexual tales of what went on behind closed doors at Mount Carmel may have comprised the core of the "Sinful Messiah" series, but guns proved to be the meat of the ATF's investigation and the ultimate catalyst for the February 28, 1993 raid on Mount Carmel. Before the Waco Siege, the ATF was probably the least known of the other "alphabet soup" federal police agencies – FBI, IRS, DEA, etc. – because it was usually not in any news reports and up until that time, was not involved in many high profile cases. Since the ATF played such a large role in the tragic events of 1993, a brief background of the agency is warranted.

The ATF was originally formed as an enforcement arm of the United States Department of Treasury and played a major role in the 1920s as the Bureau of Prohibition. After Prohibition, the Bureau of Prohibition became the Alcohol Tax Unit (ATU) of the Bureau of Internal Revenue. The ATU focused mainly on enforcing tax laws concerning the sales of alcohol and tobacco, but when the Gun Control Act of 1968 was passed, its focus switched to firearms and it became the Bureau of Alcohol, Tobacco and Firearms in 1972. After the September 11, 2001 terrorist attacks, the ATF was reorganized once more and became part of the Justice Department where it still sits today. Throughout its history, although much smaller than the FBI, the ATF has enjoyed the availability of resources that has allowed it to investigate and arrest thousands of violators of American gun laws.

In 1992 the ATF set its sights on the Branch Davidians.

The Case Opens

The ATF's case against David Koresh and the Branch Davidians officially began on July 9, 1992 after a United Parcel Service driver reported that he delivered a box of hand grenades to Mount Carmel. Although the grenades were later determined to be "dummies" and perfectly legal, the report was enough to initiate a case against the sect. There had also been reports of automatic gunfire emanating from Mount Carmel so the combination proved to be enough for the ATF to marshal its resources and send undercover agents to the region in order to infiltrate the group. The investigation of the Branch Davidians was headed by ATF special agent Davy Aguilera, who made it his personal mission to shut the group down.

The ATF rented a house about a mile down the road from Mount Carmel where it set up special agent Robert Rodriguez – posing as Robert Gonzalez – and a few other agents to pose as local area college students and win the confidence of Koresh. Almost immediately the undercover operation was flawed. Most of the agents were well into their thirties and none of them knew much about the places they claimed to come from or the professions they asserted they had.

None of this was lost on Koresh and the other Davidians.

Since Rodriguez and the other agents were investigating the Davidians for firearms violations, their mission was to gather evidence of illegal firearms and if possible purchase some. Rodriguez feigned interest in Koresh's theological messages in order to gain access to the guns, which Koresh openly showed him at Mount Carmel's shooting range. Koresh later invited Rodriguez to shoot guns at the range, who then brought his own gun, despite telling Koresh earlier he had little experience with firearms. Before his death Koresh related the event to some of his followers: "Anyway, you know, the guy's the guy's telling me . . . that he really doesn't know that much about guns, and, that the very first thing he does is he brings over this weapon that, you know, no novice has."

Koresh and the other Davidians quickly concluded that Rodriguez and his roommates were probably law enforcement; Koresh actually thought that they were probably with the Immigration and Naturalization Service (INS) there to pick up foreign Davidians who had overstayed their visas. They did not suspect that the potential convert was a special agent with the ATF.

Special agent Rodriguez was raised a Catholic, but he would later admit that his visits to Mount Carmel made him question some of his core theological beliefs. Rodriguez was taken in by Koresh's passion and charisma and as it turns out, despite knowing that he was a member of some type of government agency, Koresh hoped to convert the man to his cause.

A Weak Case

The ATF's investigation was predicated on a potential stockpile of semi-automatic rifles that were illegally converted to automatic. ATF affidavits that were later released to the public reveal that the agency knew it would have a difficult time securing a warrant to arrest Koresh so it took an approach that gave credence to any report of malfeasance at Mount Carmel, no matter the credibility.

Besides the reports of automatic gunfire coming from Mount Carmel's shooting range, which was investigated and closed by the local sheriff's department, a picture was painted of potential drug problems by Branch Davidian members. It was stated that Mount Carmel may have been the setting for a meth lab and that several members had convictions for drug offenses. The reality is that only a few members had *arrests* for minor marijuana possession charges and that there was never any evidence of illicit drugs on the grounds of Mount Carmel. True to SDA beliefs, Koresh forbade the use of illegal drugs and only later, as noted above, allowed some alcohol use on its grounds.

Branch Davidian David Thibodeaux, who survived the siege, best summed up Koresh's philosophy towards illicit drugs. "Everyone knew David Koresh hated drugs. Charges that we were assembling an arsenal of weapons to be used against the government were equally off-base. We had nothing to hide. In fact, weeks before the raid, Koresh offered the ATF the opportunity to come out to Mount Carmel and inspect the compound."

The reality is that the Branch Davidians did in fact own quite a large arsenal of guns, but there were monetary reasons for owning them.

Koresh and follower Paul Fatta became regulars on the Texas gun show circuit during the late 1980s and early 1990s. The men were strong believers in the Second Amendment and believed that they would need them when the prophecies of Revelation came to fruition. Koresh and the Davidians also learned that there was money to be made buying and selling guns at gun shows.

The Branch Davidians supported themselves through a number of means: some individuals worked jobs in Waco, the community owned an auto shop down the road from Mount Carmel, and they sold much of the land surrounding Mount Carmel at a nice profit; but Koresh learned that one of the quickest and most lucrative ways to support the community was by selling guns.

The gun business was usually brisk in Texas, but it became increasingly so after Democrat Bill Clinton was elected president of the United States, which signaled to many gun owners that the talk of an assault weapon ban would become reality within a matter of months. So in the months leading up to the Waco Siege Koresh and the Branch Davidians became involved in even more gun deals. The ATF believed that it would catch Koresh committing a firearms violation during one of his many transactions at gun shows.

Gun shows and person to person purchases are often viewed by gun control advocates as a loophole that criminals can use to illegally purchase firearms, but licensed gun dealers are required to keep records of all transactions, which are subject to investigation by the ATF. One particular person that Koresh did a lot of business with was a non-Davidian gun dealer named Henry McMahon. The ATF began investigating

McMahon under the premise that he had made either illegal or undocumented gun deals with Koresh. The ATF thoroughly searched McMahon's home and records and could find no crime; while the ATF was conducting its search, McMahon was able to call Koresh.

"If there's a problem, tell them to come out here. If they want to see my guns, they're more than welcome," Koresh said to McMahon on the phone. The agents declined to speak with Koresh or visit Mount Carmel.

The scene was set for the February raid.

CHAPTER 5:
February 28, 1993

Operation Trojan Horse/Showtime

On February 28, 1993 the ATF conducted one of the largest raids in its history and what would become its greatest tragedy. Codenamed "Operation Trojan Horse", the agents involved referred to the operation colloquially as "Showtime."

The Trojan Horse described in the ancient Roman writer Virgil's poem *The Aeneid* was used by the Mycenaeans to stealthily enter the impregnable city of Troy; but in 1993 the ATF used a "dynamic entry" to serve a warrant on Koresh. The operation involved seventy five ATF agents who were to raid Mount Carmel with automatic guns and body armor at 9:45 am, but an examination reveals that the raid was flawed before it even began.

Even though the ATF never turned up any serious violations on Koresh during its investigation, the collection of witness statements and innuendos was enough to obtain a felony arrest warrant from a federal judge. Although the warrant allowed for agents to enter the premises of Mount Carmel, it was not a "no knock" warrant, which meant that agents were legally required to identify themselves as law enforcement before entering the premises; this would later become one of many points of contention as the Branch Davidians claimed that the agents never identified themselves, while the agents claimed they did.

But even before the ATF served its warrant on Koresh at Mount Carmel it had plenty of opportunities to nab the leader.

As noted above, Koresh and the Branch Davidians knew that they were under investigation, but they also seemed to either not care or thought that nothing would come of the investigation. In the days prior to the February 28 raid, after the ATF had obtained the warrant to arrest Koresh, the sect leader left Mount Carmel several times to run errands and jog on the dirt roads in the area. Why Koresh was not arrested on one of these occasions still remains one of the most enduring unanswered questions surrounding the case.

The Gun Battle

One of the most replayed images from the Waco Siege is the gun battle between ATF agents and Branch Davidians that took place on the roof of Mount Carmel. Americans were shocked as they watched law enforcement officers exchange gunfire with the well-armed Davidians and even more shocked when they saw agents get shot and fall off the roof. The gun battle on the rooftop was only part of the overall battle and actually happened after an initial firefight took place at Mount Carmel's front door.

One of the primary controversies concerning the Waco Siege and one that has spawned numerous conspiracy theories that still resonates today, concerns who fired the first shots. The ATF claims that as they approached the front doors and identified themselves they were immediately fired upon from inside Mount Carmel. The Branch Davidians counter that the ATF agents fired first and never identified themselves. Obviously there is a large gap between the two sides, although both agree that the first shots were fired *through* the front doors.

Koresh suffered gunshot wounds from the raid, but lived and gave several statements throughout the subsequent siege. When Koresh's attorney asked why he fired on federal agents he answered: "I don't care who they are. Nobody is going to come to my home, with my babies around, without a gun back in their face. That's just the American way."

A detailed forensic investigation may have been able to reveal who shot first if the only gunshot holes in the door were punched in one way or another: if the holes were punched outside in then the ATF shot first and if vice versa then it was the Branch Davidians. Unfortunately, the door was destroyed by combat vehicles the FBI used in the April 19 raid and it has never been recovered. Two lawyers that represented a Branch Davidian who died on April 19 claimed that the only gunshot holes they noticed on the door were punched in when they visited their client during the siege. Since their client died during the siege, one could argue that they had no reason to lie. The missing door fueled many conspiracy theories and continues to do so as proponents of such ideas argue that the door was purposely destroyed to conceal evidence that would have absolved the Branch Davidians. Without the door as evidence, at this point it is impossible to say for sure who fired first. As the first shots took place at the entrance to Mount Carmel, helicopters were buzzing overhead, potentially firing shots to back up ATF agents on the ground.

Death from Above?

Both during the initial raid on Mount Carmel on February 28 and during the subsequent siege, several military grade helicopters were used by the government. The legality, or possible illegality of such a maneuver will be discussed more below, but the ATF claims that they only used the vehicles for observation during the initial raid. The explanation seems entirely plausible, but witnesses claim that several shots were fired from more than one of the helicopters.

Many of the surviving Branch Davidians claimed that the helicopters strafed Mount Carmel and were responsible for the death of a member who was on the water tower when the hostilities began. Surviving Branch Davidian member Marjorie Thomas, who actually testified for the prosecution against other surviving Davidians said in court: "As the helicopter drew nearer, I heard a sound. It was a bullet coming – which came through the window and shattered the blinds."

One can certainly argue that the word of a Branch Davidian, even if a prosecution witness, may be questionable under these circumstances, but objective witnesses and forensic evidence appears to corroborate Thomas' testimony.

When the ATF raided Mount Carmel on the morning of February 28, 1993 the *Waco Tribune* was not the only media outlet privy to the information. A number of other local and state media outlets were alerted of the impending raid and present when the shooting commenced. Among those present were reporter John McLemore and cameraman Dan Mulloney, who would both later testify that they witnessed shots coming from a helicopter. Forensic evidence seems to confirm what the two objective witnesses claimed to have seen.

The body of the Branch Davidian who was shot to death on Mount Carmel's water tower, Peter Gent, was sent to the local county coroner for a full autopsy. The coroner, who was not affiliated with either the Davidians or the federal government, concluded that the shot that killed Gent came from a level trajectory. Since the water tower was several feet above the highest point on Mount Carmel and no ATF agent scaled the tower, the only explanation is that the shot came from one of the helicopters.

It seems the jury in the Branch Davidians' criminal trial agreed. Although members of the jury stated that they believed shots did in fact come from at least one helicopter and that the ATF probably fired the first shots at the front door, they were more than likely accidental and done out of fear. This may very well be the case, but either way the ATF does not look good. If they fired first because they were overzealous then many of the conspiracy theorists seem justified when they argue the government was out of control at Waco and if they argue the ATF fired the first shots out of fear then they look like a poorly disciplined organization that has no business being in law enforcement.

Although the ATF may have lied about firing the first shots and the extent to which they used helicopters, the Branch Davidians were also not above twisting the truth to their purpose.

During the fifty one day siege, Koresh claimed that a child had been killed in Mount Carmel during the initial siege of February 28. It is true that a number of children did die in Mount Carmel on April 19, but after extensive record searches and interviews with survivors it now appears that the "phantom child" that Koresh spoke about during the siege was merely a ploy intended to garner sympathy. Koresh also claimed that ATF agents killed Branch Davidian Perry Jones during the raid, but an autopsy revealed that he was probably killed by friendly fire from his fellow Davidians. Despite the legal and emotional issues surrounding the shootout at the front door and from the helicopters, it was the firefight on the roof of Mount Carmel that etched an image in so many people's minds.

The Botched Rooftop Entry

The ATF raid on Mount Carmel was to be essentially three tiered: a group of agents would storm the front simultaneously with another group scaling the side of the building and then entering through a rooftop window, while the helicopters hovered for support. The logic was that the group entering through the roof would seize any weapons the Branch Davidians had stored before they had a chance to use them, thereby affecting a successful arrest.

Of course, things do not always go as planned.

The agents who conducted the rooftop raid were brought to their target by pickup trucks pulling cattle cars that contained the agents and ladders they used to scale the walls of Mount Carmel. At first the maneuver seemed to work well, but when the first three agents went into the complex through a rooftop window they were met with heavy resistance. Surviving agents claim that shots came from all directions, which appears plausible since the walls of Mount Carmel were constructed with cheap plywood. The walls would not have been able to even slow down any bullets so the Branch Davidians could have shot through walls once they knew the ATF was attempting to enter. The video footage proves as much, as shots came from the inside out; but the video also proves that the Branch Davidians did not fire first on the rooftop. The confusion of the firefight inside was probably further exacerbated by the "flash bang" grenades that the agents used.

The video footage also shows that one of the ATF shot himself in the leg while climbing a ladder, which demonstrates the uncontrollable and dangerous nature of such a large operation.

The agents inside were forced to retreat and ultimately three of them died either on the roof or from wounds sustained in the attempted entry. A total of four ATF agents died on February 28, 1993

The Ceasefire

After nearly two hours of shooting, the ATF called a ceasefire to their operations around 11:30 am. Koresh and the Davidians agreed and let the ATF carry off their four dead and fourteen wounded agents. Immediately after the shooting began,

Branch Davidian and lawyer, Wayne Martin, called 911 and was put through to Lieutenant Larry Lynch of the local sheriff's department. Of course there was nothing that Lynch could do to stop the gunfire, but was a voice of authority that Koresh and his followers were willing to speak with; that is when the FBI allowed the calls to go through.

As the images of the February 28 shootout began to filter throughout the United States and then the world, questions were immediately raised by concerned citizens.

At press conferences after the initial raid, spokespeople for the ATF often appeared flustered and unable to answer simple questions. The ATF spent months preparing for the raid on Mount Carmel, but apparently never considered contingency plans or how to deal with the public if things went wrong, as they did. Often it was local reporters who asked questions such as why Koresh was not arrested on one of the numerous occasions when he left the compound and why was there a need for a "dynamic entry" in the first place.

More skeptical citizens pointed out that the ATF was due to face a congressional budget hearing in a matter of months – was the raid done to publicly justify its existence? Of course the ATF denied any connection between the raid on Mount Carmel and the impending budget hearing; but once the question was let out of Pandora's Box, it was impossible to put it back in.

CHAPTER 6:
The Siege

The FBI Takes Over

After the events of February 28, the federal government licked its wounds, prepared for a siege, and turned over command to the FBI. The FBI was better prepared for such an operation as it had more manpower, resources, and prestige. The superior resources of the FBI allowed it to have its own specially trained swat team – the Hostage Recovery Team (HRT) – and agents who were trained specifically as crisis negotiators. The FBI was also much more of a "brand name" than the ATF. In 1993 virtually every American knew what the FBI was, unlike the ATF, and most people had a relatively positive view of the agency – they investigated and arrested bank robbers, gangsters, and even spies. But by the time the FBI became involved in the Waco Siege it had recently suffered its own public relations debacle.

During the summer of 1992, the FBI became involved in a standoff with a white separatist named Randy Weaver at a place called Ruby Ridge in northern Idaho. Weaver had sold an illegally altered shotgun (too much of the barrel had been sawed off) to an informant for the ATF, which led to the ATF attempting to turn him into an informant. When Weaver refused, he was charged with a felony. Eventually, after nearly two years, the United States Marshals attempted to perform an arrest on Weaver, but the agents failed to identify themselves, which resulted in a shootout that left a Marshal dead and Weaver's fourteen year old son Samuel shot to death in the back. In the Weaver case, like the Waco Siege, the FBI was called in, which resulted in more death when FBI sniper Lon Horiuchi shot and killed Weaver's wife, Vicki. Weaver and family friend Kevin Harris were charged with the murder of the Marshal, but eventually cleared of all charges. Interestingly, Horiuchi was also present at the Waco Siege.

By most accounts the FBI did not want the events at Mount Carmel to turn into another Ruby Ridge, but fault lines within the FBI were apparent immediately. Two schools of thought were prevalent within the ranks of the FBI: the negotiators appeared to favor a long-term approach, while others, such as the HRT members, wished to carry out another raid on Mount Carmel.

Any attempts to end the siege peacefully seemed doomed from the start.

Signs of Hope?

Despite the fissures within the FBI from the beginning of the siege, there were early signs from within Mount Carmel that the siege might end peacefully. Koresh told FBI negotiators that he would surrender if his interpretation of the Seven Seals was made public. The prophet spoke with reporters from the Cable News Network (CNN) and local radio station KRLD early during the siege about some of his ideas concerning the Seals and stated that if they publicized his interpretation of all of them, then he would end the siege.

A number of Branch Davidians also left Mount Carmel in the early part of the siege.

Twenty one children and fourteen adults left, which most people saw as a good sign.

There seemed to be an exodus taking place from Mount Carmel, but then it stopped. Most of the children who stayed were Koresh's and the followers that stayed were his most loyal. They were not afraid of death as to them that would only fulfill the prophecies that Koresh preached in his sermons. The resolve of those who stayed was hardened even further when they later learned that the adults who surrendered were charged with sundry felonies and the children were sent to foster care. Also, Koresh began to vacillate concerning his message and if he would even reveal it if given the chance.

The scene was set for a long-term siege.

The FBI Attempts to End the Siege

As the siege at Waco turned from days into weeks, many in the government became anxious and searched for ways to end it. Eventually, the school of thought within the FBI that favored another raid eventually triumphed, but it appears that it was more of a process to arrive there than a sudden decision.

One of the first things the FBI did was to send in "bugs" and other listening devices with milk for the remaining children and medical supplies for the wounded, such as Koresh. The devices did not reveal much other than the Branch Davidians were a bit hungry and tired, but no attack or mass suicide plans were heard. As the FBI listened for any weaknesses within Mount Carmel, they used a number of tactics in order to sow discord from outside the compound.

One of the first tactics the FBI used was turning the phone lines and power at Mount Carmel on and off intermittently. To many people today, especially those under the age of thirty, the idea of a "land line" phone may seem foreign, but in 1993 they were vital for communication. Although Koresh did own a cellular phone and it was used throughout the siege, cell phones need power and if the power is cut then the phone cannot be charged. Also, cell phone coverage in 1993 was extremely spotty because there were far fewer cell towers as not many people owned cell phones. The FBI did not want the Branch Davidians to contact their friends and allies on the outside world, so the phone was only turned on when they needed to speak with Koresh. Overall, the limited phone usage meant that not only were the Branch Davidians not able to contact their supporters, but Koresh was not able to contact media outlets with his message. After the first few days, the FBI severely restricted Koresh's contact with the media.

When the FBI cut the power to Mount Carmel it had less of a negative effect than intended. For the most part, the Branch Davidians lived a fairly austere life in the confines of Mount Carmel – there was no central heat or air conditioning and few appliances – so being without electricity did not bother them much. Soon the FBI learned that their sporadic power outages were having little effect so they decided to try psychological operations.

Psychological operations have been employed by governments since the beginning of civilization, but were brought to a much higher level during the Cold War. Intelligence organizations like the CIA and KGB experimented with live human subjects in order to determine if tactics like sleep deprivation could influence a person's decision making. During the Waco Siege, the FBI employed a number of these tactics.

At night the FBI would use flood lights to wake up the residents of Mount Carmel and during the day various rock songs and sound effects were broadcast at extremely high decibels. For the most part, it appears that the Branch Davidians took most of those psychological operations in stride as they responded by holding jam sessions in order to drown out the sounds from the outside. As the siege wore on though, the psychological operations became more ominous.

As negotiations appeared to break down and FBI agents became more frustrated, they began to use military vehicles to circle Mount Carmel. Helicopters returned for these maneuvers, but it was the tanks that were the most menacing as they rolled over cars and other small structures on the grounds of Mount Carmel. The legality of the government's use of military vehicles for these maneuvers, as well as during the February 28 and April 19 raids was raised by numerous people during the Waco Siege and in the years since.

The Posse Comitatus Act

In many countries throughout the world, especially in the developing world, there is often a blurred line between the police and military; but in the United States the line has always been clear and distinct. The separation between the military and police that exists in American culture is partly due to the existence of the Third Amendment to the United States Constitution, which prohibits the quartering of soldiers in private citizens' homes. The philosophy can also be traced more directly to an 1878 federal law.

The Posse Comitatus Act of 1878 expressly prohibits the military from taking part in domestic police actions. Although the law seems fairly straightforward, it has been skirted numerous times in recent decades. During the civil disturbances of the 1960s the national guard of the various states was used to quell riots and since the 1970s the Drug Enforcement Agency (DEA) has used military equipment and advisors in a number of their raids. These actions have been legally challenged and upheld by the Supreme Court, as it has argued that in those situations a limited military involvement is justified. Lawyers for the Branch Davidians and various legal scholars have argued the ATF and FBI's use of military equipment was a clear violation of the Posse Comitatus Act, but those agencies contend that it was not.

As discussed above, both the ATF and FBI used military helicopters and tanks during the Waco Siege and as was revealed in court, the ATF agents received training from Green Berets before the ill-fated February 28 raid. After the siege, the FBI claimed that it was authorized to use that equipment under a 1989 federal law that allows the military to train police for drug raids. Both agencies claim that the potential drug use and manufacturing at Mount Carmel justified the military presence, but again, no evidence of such activity was ever shown. The use of military equipment by both the ATF and FBI at Waco continues to raise serious legal questions, but an examination of the negotiation tactics by the FBI also reveals some serious flaws in the agency's crisis strategy.

The FBI Works against Itself

As David Koresh vacillated concerning when and if he would release his interpretation of the Seven Seals, the FBI seemed to show no clear strategy as to how it would end the crisis. One day the FBI would use psychological operations and the next it would call Koresh on the phone and invite him to discuss his theological beliefs – there was clearly a disconnect going on within the Bureau. The FBI's own behavioral scientists warned that an aggressive approach – such as psychological operations, especially the more aggressive ones with military equipment – would only add to the Branch Davidians' resolve and possibly escalate the situation into more violence. The faction of the FBI represented by the HRT did not seem to care, while the negotiators who did seem to genuinely want to end the standoff peacefully never took the time to understand the Branch Davidians' fundamental beliefs.

Biblical scholars, such as James D. Tabor, were called in by the FBI negotiators in order to better understand Branch Davidian theology, but they claim they were ignored for the most part and were never allowed a direct conversation with Koresh.

Tabor later said that most agents believed that the Seven Seals were "seagoing creatures with whiskers" and did not care to learn even the basics of the theology.

Time was running out and the HRT faction of the FBI had come into the ascendancy.

CHAPTER 7:
Outside Support for the Davidians

Constitutionalists and Right Wing Populists

As the Waco Siege wore on, despite the FBI's best efforts, Koresh and the Branch Davidians began to garner a fair amount of support across the United States. Some support came from the mainstream SDA Church, but most of the more vocal advocates were not of the same faith as Koresh and his followers. One of the more vociferous groups of people to support the Branch Davidians can be defined collectively as "constitutionalists." There was not then, or now, one single group or organization that claims to speak for all constitutionalists and the very definition of who, or what, a constitutionalist is, is actually somewhat amorphous.

For the most part, constitutionalists adhere to a strict interpretation of the United States constitution, especially the first ten amendments, also known as the Bill of Rights. In fact, many constitutionalists disregard any amendment after the Tenth, as they see those as incursions on freedom and political rights. Constitutionalists are almost always on the right wing of the political spectrum, but with a more populist and often anti-government tone to their messages. Many constitutionalists were popular on AM talk radio in 1993 and that is where they spread their message of support for the Branch Davidians and condemnation of the federal government.

From their radio studio pulpits, constitutionalist talk show hosts often pointed out that they did not agree with the Branch Davidians' theological ideas and certainly not any sexual improprieties by Koresh, if in fact any happened, but that the Davidians had a right to "life, liberty, and the pursuit of happiness" as stated in the Declaration of Independence. In particular, constitutionalists argued that the Branch Davidians' First Amendment rights were violated because their freedom of assembly and association was trounced upon by both the ATF and FBI. Most Constitutionalists also argued that the Branch Davidians Second Amendment rights were violated and some of the more fiery ones stated that the raid may be the beginning of a general gun confiscation by the federal government – unless Americans stood up.

Local Community Members

While Constitutionalists and right wing populists disseminated their messages of support for the Branch Davidians and condemnation of the federal government, more and more people began to turn up at the media camp outside Mount

Carmel. Slowly but surely the camp began to take on a carnival type atmosphere, where people from all over the United States publicly stated their support for the besieged Branch Davidians and their disgust with the federal government.

But what about the people from the Waco area?

Opinions concerning support for the Branch Davidians or the federal government in the local community varied. Waco, like most of Texas outside of Austin, is fairly conservative, which means that they have a strong belief in God and guns. Waco is home to Baylor University, the largest and most prestigious Southern Baptist University in the United States, and is a place where gun shops are as common as hair salons. Waco is also home to a relatively high percentage of military veterans and is close to the U.S. Army base, Fort Hood. Because of these factors the opinions among the people of Waco were actually varied and there does not seem to have been a consensus.

Most people believed that the Branch Davidians had a right to practice religion as they saw fit, as long as it was within the confines of the law, and that their supposedly large arsenal was no big deal. On the other hand, most of the people of Waco supported the government and believed that for the ATF to conduct such a high profile raid then the Branch Davidians must have done something wrong.

Among the core who believed that the Branch Davidians were essentially just eccentrics that were unfairly targeted were those who knew the members personally. One local Waco resident, Keith Ellis, told a reporter that "the sneak attack was wrong," in reference to the February 28 raid. Other locals, such as Dennis Moore, felt the need to qualify the Branch Davidians' existence as a legitimate religious organization. "We always referred to it as a religious commune, not a cult," said Moore to reporters. Although Moore was technically an outsider to the Davidians, he owned a bar that some members frequented as stand in musicians. Despite garnering a certain amount of support from locals who knew them, the Branch Davidians also picked up their fair share of detractors during the Waco Siege.

Besides people who believed the government narrative that the Branch Davidians were the ones to blame for the situation at Mount Carmel, a number of locals began to tire of the media circus and the negative image that they believed was being foisted upon Waco. As a result, both those who tired of the situation and the people who believed the government narrative coalesced to offer financial and moral support to government agents.

The Waco Siege quickly brought hundreds of federal agents and media personnel to the metro Waco area, but as the siege wore on there was a lack of housing among other things. Many local area businesses stepped in and offered free meals and housing to visiting agents.

These local residents wanted the Waco Siege to end quickly so that they could get back to their normal lives.

Other Branch Davidian Supporters

Besides the Constitutionalists and local residents who knew the Branch Davidians, a number of random supporters materialized, both at Mount Carmel and throughout the country, who supported the Branch Davidians for a plethora of reasons. Some supporters expressed genuine sympathy for the suffering of the Davidians, especially the children, while others did so for theological and political reasons. The disparate coalition can hardly be defined as a group, but some interesting and historically important developments took place within their ranks during the fifty one day siege.

Ken Fawcett and Ken Engelman were two men who supported the Branch Davidians from a primarily humanitarian standpoint. In early 1993, Fawcett was a communications technician in the Waco area and Engelman was the host of a radio show on local station KGBS. Although Engleman's show took a decidedly conservative stance on most political issues, he was certainly not an anti-government zealot. Through their jobs, the two men devised a simple way to communicate with the Branch Davidians.

As mentioned above, as the siege wore on the FBI essentially eliminated the Branch Davidians' ability to communicate with the outside world. Fawcett, who had been keeping track of the siege through live feeds, noticed a satellite dish on top of Mount Carmel. Fawcett devised a communication method whereby someone would ask the Branch Davidians simple questions that they would then answer by moving the dish a certain way. Fawcett brought the idea to Engelman, who believed that Koresh and his followers may have been listening to his show via a battery powered radio.

"David, if you can hear my voice, move your satellite dish from Galaxy 6 to Galaxy 1," asked Fawcett on Engelman's show. The dish soon moved to the appropriate position, which told the two men that they had effectively established contact with Mount Carmel. The two men continued to communicate with the Branch Davidians throughout the siege using the simple method. Fawcett and Engelman's support for the Branch Davidians was rooted in humanitarian grounds, but a number of supporters distinguished themselves for theological reasons.

Although the Branch Davidians were a relatively small sect, they were associated with the SDA Church, which has millions of adherents worldwide. For the most part, the mainline SDA leaders tried to distance themselves from Koresh and the events at Mount Carmel, but some notable theologians emerged to give their support to the besieged Branch

Davidians. Philip Arnold and James Tabor both gave interviews to the media where they stated that ideas promulgated by Koresh were for the most part biblically sound. Tabor in particular attempted to mediate between the FBI and the Branch Davidians but was rebuffed by the former. Among the religious supporters of the Branch Davidians was one young Texan who nearly got himself killed in his attempt to show solidarity with the inhabitants of Mount Carmel.

Louis Alaniz was a twenty five year old from Houston when the Waco Siege began. Like many men his age, much of his time was spent trying to find meaning in his life and his place in the world. When the raid on February 28 took place he intently watched the events unfold along with millions of other Americans; but unlike most other Americans, the Waco Siege gave Alaniz an epiphany and his life suddenly had meaning. Alaniz took a Greyhound bus from Houston to Waco, where he then hitchhiked as close as he could get to Mount Carmel.

The young man crawled through fields and ravines and somehow made it through the canvass of law enforcement officers that killed a Branch Davidian earlier in the siege who was trying to make it to Mount Carmel. Once at Mount Carmel, Alaniz frantically knocked on what was left of the front door as federal agents demanded that he surrender. The Branch Davidians eventually opened the door where they then cleaned up Alaniz, gave him some of their meagre food rations, and sat him down to speak with Koresh. After listening to a lengthy theological discourse from Koresh, Alaniz left Mount Carmel, which happened to be the day before the final assault took place.

Finally, a number of more militant political activists began to assemble around the media camp outside Mount Carmel. Most of these activists were there not so much to support the Branch Davidians, but more so to show their disdain for the federal government. Most of these people were men and a few had also been at the Ruby Ridge, Idaho standoff a few months earlier. Many of these men were members of the nascent militia movement that exponentially grew in the months after the Waco Siege. A few of them related to the media their conspiracy theories that involved "black helicopters", marshal law, and the United Nations.

Among the anti-government activists gathered outside Mount Carmel was a twenty four year old United States Army veteran named Tim McVeigh who distributed bumper stickers that read, "Is Your Church ATF-Approved?"

CHAPTER 8:
April 19, 1993

Jumping the Gun?

After nearly two months of on again, off again talks between David Koresh and FBI negotiators, the HRT wing of the FBI finally won – they decided to use force to extricate the Branch Davidians from Mount Carmel: but did the FBI act too soon?

Evidence shows that Koresh and his followers may have been ready to leave when the FBI assault took place. True to their SDA Old Testament practices, the inhabitants of Mount Carmel were observing Passover, which happened to end on April 14 in 1993. Shortly after the Branch Davidians' observance of Passover ended, Koresh told the FBI that god had given him permission to write his interpretation of the Seven Seals and that once he was done, he and the remaining Davidians would surrender. He completed the First Seal on April 16, which seemed to indicate the rest would quickly follow.

The FBI negotiators were pleased with Koresh's statement, but FBI agents who favored a raid argued that it was just a stall technique and pointed out that Koresh had reneged on previous claims that he would surrender. There were also other influences that pushed the FBI towards the final assault.

Bill Clinton was a new president and as a Democrat – who are often seen as weaker on crime and terrorism than Republicans – did not want to be held hostage by a religious extremist in Texas. Clinton gave full authority to his Attorney General, Janet Reno, to resolve the standoff any way she saw fit, which included force. Reno later absolved Clinton of any impropriety during the Waco Siege by stating, "the buck stops here", which effectively distanced the president from any negative fall out, but why she gave the green light for the April 19 assault has never been completely answered.

It is true that a faction of the FBI favored a tactical assault on Mount Carmel from the beginning, but outside influences may explain why the pro-negotiation faction of the FBI and Janet Reno acquiesced and authorized the assault. Many scholars of the Waco Siege point towards the efforts of a group called the Cult Awareness Network (CAN) that painted a picture of the Branch Davidians that still resonates in the minds of many people. The CAN advised the FBI that by all definitions the Branch Davidians were a millennial or doomsday cult and that there was no way Koresh would relinquish his grip on the group to the government. CAN advisors argued that the longer the FBI waited, the greater the chance Mount Carmel would end in a mass suicide similar to the one that took place in Jonestown, Guyana in 1978.

CAN's influence proved to be decisive – the raid was scheduled for six a.m. on April 19.

The Final Assault Begins

The Branch Davidians who were actually sleeping at six a.m. on April 19 were awoken to sounds of combat engineering vehicles (CEVs) clearing the vehicles and small building that had not already been destroyed by the FBI during the fifty one day siege. The CEVs quickly completed their first task and then turned to the primary and most controversial task that they would be used for that day – the insertion of CS gas into Mount Carmel.

CS gas is the abbreviated name for the chemical orthochlorobenzalmalononitrile, more common known by its vernacular name, "tear gas." Most people are familiar to some extent with CS gas as it is commonly used by police forces throughout the world to disperse riots and sometimes as a non-lethal tactic to detain violent suspects. Most people are not aware of some of the hazardous side effects of the gas and its unstable nature, particularly how it can easily become flammable.

During World War I, both the Allies and Central Powers experimented with weaponized poisonous gas to widely ranging results. For the most part, weaponized poisonous gas proved to be an unstable and unpredictable weapon: for instance, weaponized gas launched at an enemy could be caught by winds and exposed to the side that launched it. The effects of poison gas during World War I became well publicized and because of that, along with it negligible effectiveness, a majority of the world's nations, including the United States, banned their use in war. CS was included in the ban, but as David Thibodeaux pointed out: "Apparently there is no prohibition against its use against American citizens." Thibodeaux's statement, although cynical, is for the most part correct; but its use by police agencies in the United States is usually very controlled and done only under specific settings.

As noted above, CS gas is usually used in outdoor settings to prevent riots and when used indoors, small amounts are usually used by a minimum of officers. In enclosed spaces CS gas can cause severe respiratory problems to those exposed and converts into the deadly poison cyanide when it burns. Essentially, CS gas can become an extremely deadly chemical when used indoors in high amounts.

The FBI used two methods to disperse the CS gas into Mount Carmel: hand-held grenade launchers, similar to what are used to control riots throughout the world, were used to launch more than 400 "ferret rounds" of gas into the building and CEVs punched holes into the building's walls and then sprayed a form of the gas that was suspended in methylene chloride. A stream of carbon dioxide was used as a dispersant in order to further spread the gas throughout the complex.

Most of the FBI agents who dispersed the gas into Mount Carmel on April 19 probably did not know its potential side effects; but the amount they used ensured that tragedy would unfold.

The Fire

Almost as soon as the CS gas was inserted into Mount Carmel, multiple fires broke out throughout the complex. Infrared camera footage taken from helicopters released by the government after the assault shows that the fires broke out nearly simultaneously on different levels and in completely different areas of Mount Carmel. The government argued this this partially proved that Koresh and his most ardent followers lit these fires themselves in one last attempt to fulfill the apocalyptic prophecy. The government also argued that transcripts from the bugging devices they placed in Mount Carmel prove the Branch Davidians intentionally set the fires.

Transcribing recorded conversations and interviews is more of an art than a science. Specific accents, mumbling, and background noises all have to be considered when one transcribes an audio recording, which can be difficult in a simple conversation, never mind a pitched battle. In various parts of the audio tapes from April 19, the government transcribed Koresh saying "light the fire," but defense attorneys for surviving Branch Davidians argued that most of the recordings were inaudible. One may argue that defense attorneys are not the most objective people, but more recently, noted scholar Catherine Wessinger listened to the tapes as part of her own research on the Waco Siege and concluded that the files were inaudible. Although the audio evidence may be inconclusive concerning whether or not the Branch Davidians set the fire, the FBI argued that physical evidence also points towards their guilt.

"Nine Branch Davidians exited that compound that last day. Seven of the nine had accelerants on their clothing," said FBI chief negotiator Byron Sage when questioned about the origins of the massive fire that consumed Mount Carmel. This evidence would surely point towards the Davidians' guilt, but defense attorneys for the inhabitants of Mount Carmel, as well as various scholars of the Waco Siege, have pointed out that many chemicals can be considered an "accelerant." As noted above, Mount Carmel lacked central heating so space heaters were often used and when the FBI cut the power to the facility, its inhabitants relied on the highly flammable chemical kerosene for most of the standoff for heat.

If the Branch Davidians did set the fire themselves then it would point towards a mass suicide scenario, which experts from the CAN warned the FBI would happen. If a mass suicide were to have happened, then one would expect to find all of the Branch Davidians gathered in one place, probably the chapel, but this was not the case. In fact, the only place where any significant number of Branch Davidians died in one place was what they believed was a fireproof vault. The vault is where the remains of most of the children and their mothers' were found, which does not suggest the actions of a suicidal people. The Branch Davidians were well stocked with survival equipment, which included gas masks, but unfortunately for the children there was no size that could fit them. Surviving Branch Davidians claim that the mothers brought the children to vault because they believed it would shield them first from the gas and then the flames.

Unfortunately they were wrong.

More Evidence for CS Gas as the Cause of the Fire

It may never be known for sure where the genesis of the fire at Mount Carmel originated, but more anecdotal evidence points towards CS gas being the culprit. As noted above, CS gas has the potential to be flammable when large amounts are used in enclosed places and two specific cases seem to confirm as much.

In the early 1970s, members of a violent, highly-armed leftist revolutionary group known as the Symbionese Liberation Army went on a bank robbing and bombing spree throughout southern California. The Los Angeles Police Department finally caught up with some of the key members of the organization in 1974, who sealed themselves up in a safe house and engaged in a firefight with the police. The Los Angeles County Sheriff's Department, California Highway Patrol, and the local branch of the FBI were called in as reinforcements; the FBI supplied hundreds of canisters of CS gas. The law enforcement officers launched the gas cartridges into the house, which then caught fire, killing most of the terrorists.

The FBI encountered a similar situation in 1984. In that particular incident, a man named Robert Matthews, who was the leader of a white separatist organization called the Silent Brotherhood, barricaded himself inside a house outside of Seattle. After an intense firefight, FBI agents shot CS gas into the house, which then caught fire and burned down.

Experts point out that only three things are needed to ignite CS gas: oxygen, a combustible material, and an ignition source, all of which were readily available at Mount Carmel. Most of the material made to construct Mount Carmel was combustible and ignition sources were also plentiful: a pilot light, gunfire, or even a lighter could have set the fire off, but evidence released in 1999 reveals that the government may have inadvertently triggered the fire.

In the aftermath of the Waco Siege, criminal and civil trials, as well as congressional hearings placed new light on the tragic events of those fifty one days. One fact that came to surface was that the FBI used pyrotechnics, along with CS gas, in order to subdue the inhabitants of Mount Carmel. The explosions from the pyrotechnic charges are another possible source of the fire that consumed Mount Carmel.

As the blazing fire began to consume Mount Carmel, fire trucks from the Waco Fire Department began to arrive outside the gates of the complex around 12:20 p.m., but were halted by law enforcement officers. The firefighters are forced to watch the blaze consume Mount Carmel for over twenty more minutes before they are allowed to go to work; but by that time it was too late, Mount Carmel was a smoldering pile of ash.

Immediate Results of the April 19 Raid

The immediate fallout from the FBI raid on April 19 was severe as seventy six Branch Davidians died that day, which included twenty one children ages fifteen and younger and two fetuses. Five Branch Davidians died on February 28 during the first raid and one died that day trying to enter Mount Carmel from the outside.

The prophet, David Koresh, was among the Branch Davidians who died at Mount Carmel on April 19.

The nine Branch Davidians that survived the fire were promptly taken away and charged with an assortment of felonies, conspiracy to murder federal agents being the most severe. As the Davidians were charged, most of the evidence that could have proved their innocence, or the government's case, literally went up in smoke.

In terms of loss of life, the raid was a success for the FBI because none of their agents were killed. It also apparently invoked a sense of pride among some members and gave ATF members a feeling of retribution for the comrades they lost on February 28.

After the smoke cleared, federal agents then raised American, Texas, and ATF flags above the ruins of Mount Carmel and some even posed for pictures in front of red flags that marked where bodies of Branch Davidians were found. Not all federal agents posed for the pictures; some were visibly and vocally upset with the entire situation.

One of the immediate results of the Waco Siege was that it revealed the rift between the FBI negotiators and the HRT. According to the FBI's own statistics, 95% of all hostage-barricade incidents result in a non-lethal resolution, while tactical assaults end in injury 78% of the time. With statistics this clear and obviously available to the FBI, why the FBI opted to commit a tactical assault on April 19 continues to be a pertinent question. In the words of Gary Noesner, who was the lead FBI negotiator during the first half of the siege: "The negotiators' approach was working until they had the rug pulled out from under them."

The immediate results of the Waco Siege gave way to long-term repercussions for both everyone involved.

CHAPTER 9:
The Aftermath

The Criminal Trial of the Branch Davidians

For most of the Branch Davidians who survived the Waco Siege, their tribulations were about to begin. Norman Allison, Renos Avram, Brad Branch, Jaime Castillo, Graeme Craddock, Clive Doyle, Livingston Fagan, Paul Fatta, Woodrow Kendrick, Ruth Riddle, and Kevin Whitecliff were all charged with an assortment of felonies in federal court with conspiracy to murder federal officers and attempted murder of federal officers being the charges that carried the most time. Some survivors testified against the others for immunity from prosecution or reduced sentences, but the Branch Davidians on trial soon learned it was not former members turned prosecution witnesses, or even a biased jury that was their biggest obstacle, it was the presiding judge.

The Branch Davidians' trial took place in the United States District Court for the Western District of Texas in the city of San Antonio in January, 1994. Even before the trial began, the deck seemed to be stacked against the Branch Davidians.

Defense attorneys tried to move the trial from the overwhelming Roman Catholic location of San Antonio to no avail and in fact most pre-trial motions Judge Walter Smith ruled on seemingly worked against them.

Judge Walter Smith was fifty three years old when he presided over the Branch Davidians' trial in 1994. Smith was quite familiar with the Waco metropolitan area, as he was a graduate of Baylor Law School and practiced law in the area for a number of years. He was nominated by President Ronald Reagan to serve as a federal judge in the United States District Court for the Western District of Texas in 1984 and confirmed by the Senate that same year. Judge Smith was known for being quite conservative politically and wore his Baptist faith on his sleeve at times. Witnesses claim that he found the Branch Davidians' theology strange and their way of life odious. The several rulings he made before and during the Branch Davidians' trial appears to confirm his attitude.

One of the first and most important pre-trial motions made by defense attorneys was to sever the cases into fourteen separate trials instead of one. This is actually a common tactic used by defense attorneys when a group of defendants are charged with the same crime. Severing a trial is beneficial to the defense because, if guilty, some defendants are usually more culpable than others. Although jurors are instructed in a group trial that they can find some defendants guilty and others not guilty, the process can be confusing often the less culpable are still convicted and sentenced along with the ring leaders. Although the presumed ring leader, David Koresh, was dead, defense attorneys knew that some defendants, such as Paul Fatta who were not even at Mount Carmel during the siege, clearly had less to do with the situation than others. Also, since each defendant had his/her own attorney, severing the trials would make it logistically easier for the lawyers.

The motion was denied.

Judge Smith also denied defense subpoenas of ATF and FBI officers, who the defense argued could help clear their defendants if questioned under oath. The defense planned to ask the agents questions under oath pertaining to the lack of evidence that led to Koresh's arrest warrant, who fired first on February 28, and how much CS gas was used on April 19. Smith ruled that calling agents to the stand would possibly jeopardize their safety and any cases they were currently working on.

Finally, Smith placed a gag order on both the prosecution and the defense for the duration of the trial. Generally speaking, in criminal trials, gag orders tend to be opposed more by the defense than the prosecution. In a high profile case such as the Branch Davidian trial, the prosecution has nearly unlimited resources from the government, while the defense is forced to operate on a finite and often small budget. Speaking with the media is a good way for defense attorneys to try the case outside of the court room, which gives them a chance to gauge public opinion and modify their defense if need be.

As the trial went on, the government's case against the Branch Davidians appeared weak, especially when a number of their star witnesses gave testimony that seemingly supported the defendants. With that said, the trial did reveal that some illegal activity took place in Mount Carmel before February 28, 1993.

It was revealed that some of the guns in the Branch Davidians' arsenal had been illegally modified, which Koresh admitted to during the fifty one day siege. "Yes, I have some things maybe I shouldn't have. I mean, hey, if the Vatican can have its own little country, can't I?" said Koresh to FBI negotiators on March 7.

After both the prosecution and the defense made their final arguments, the case went to the jury, which leaned towards acquittal on most of the charges. Doyle, Allison, and Kendrick were found not guilty of all charges and the other eleven were found not guilty of the two most serious charges – conspiracy to murder federal officers and attempted murder of federal officers – but guilty on various firearms violations. Members of the jury revealed that it was a compromise verdict according to jury forewoman, Sarah Bain, who wrote: "After we had delivered our verdict to the court and prior to its being presented to the public, we jurors discussed what most of us felt was the possibility that with the consideration of time already served by the defendants, none would be facing severe penalties. Even five years is too severe a penalty for what we believed was a minor charge."

And at first judge Smith seemed to agree.

Smith ruled that if all of the defendants were found not guilty of the most serious charges, counts one and two, then count three – using and carrying a firearm during and in relation of the commission of an offense – should be thrown out since legally no crime took place. Everything seemed to work out well for both sides; some of the Branch Davidians would spend time in prison, but not the rest of their lives. Despite the tragedy of the Waco Siege, perhaps the compromise verdict would bring a certain amount of closure for both sides. But in a case as tragic and convoluted as the Waco Siege nothing was so simple and judge Smith changed his ruling.

Smith learned of a case in the same district where an inconsistent verdict was allowed to stand, which meant that when he sentenced the defendants on June 17, 1994 he essentially found the Branch Davidians guilty of the conspiracy charge they were found not guilty of by the jury. He wrote: "These defendants, and other adult Branch Davidians, engaged in a conspiracy to cause the deaths of federal agents. It was a part of the beliefs of the Branch Davidians, expressed and taught by their leader." Smith even added that it was the Davidians who shot first on February 28 – a point that was never proven in court – and that the group committed mass suicide on April 19.

Judge Smith had effectively nullified the jury's verdict.

Smith handed out sentences to the Branch Davidians that ranged in length from five to forty years, which were the type of sentences that the defense attorneys believed that they had avoided when the jury acquitted the group of the two most serious charges. Fortunately for the Branch Davidians, the Supreme Court saw the inconsistencies in judge Smith's sentencing and reduced each of the their sentences by five to twenty years in July, 2000. After serving time in federal prisons across the United States all of the surviving Branch Davidians were free by July, 2007. Although the Branch Davidians found the American justice system full of legal land mines that worked against them, they decided to use it against the government in a wrongful death lawsuit in federal court.

Unfortunately for the Branch Davidians, Judge Smith presided over their civil action against the government and for the most part he ruled in much of the same way he did in the criminal trial. He routinely denied subpoenas of federal agents the Branch Davidians called to testify and refused to allow other witnesses to testify who may have pointed the finger at the government. Not surprisingly, the jury in the civil trail found in the government's favor on July 14, 2000 and the Branch Davidians were awarded no damages. Observers and scholars have since questioned the procedures and objectivity of the judge and some have even recently called his character into question, which will be discussed below.

Congressional Hearings

In the years after the Waco Siege, a number of events took place that kept the tragedy in the public eye and continued to raise questions pertaining to the role both the government and the Branch Davidians played and if the conflict could have been avoided. Almost as soon as the criminal trial of the surviving Branch Davidians was concluded, a number of books and articles were written and documentaries were made. Many of the books and articles were written by legitimate journalists and academics such as Dick Reavis, Stuart Wright, and Catherine Wessinger who asked reasonable questions concerning the nature of the government's investigation of the Branch Davidians and their conduct during and after the siege. The legitimate scholars and journalists have also been critical of the Branch Davidians, especially David Koresh, and pointed out opportunities that they had to peacefully end the fifty one day siege. A number of credible video documentaries were also produced, such as *Waco: The Rules of Engagement* that focused on problems of the government's case against the Branch Davidians and how and why their tactics during the siege went wrong. The questions raised by these works led to two sets of congressional hearings in 1995 and 2000.

The 1995 hearings took place during the summer on the heels of the Oklahoma City bombing, which will be discussed below, and so took a decidedly pro-government tone. For the most part, the Branch Davidians were portrayed as a cult and David Koresh as their charismatic leader who ran Mount Carmel like a military camp and treated the female inhabitants, even underage girls, as his harem. Disaffected members testified to the former prophet's inequities and the large stockpile of weapons at Mount Carmel. Despite the deflection that some argued the government engaged in during the hearings, the FBI did not escape total culpability in the eyes of the committee.

The final report read: "The Attorney General knew or should have known that there was little risk to the FBI agents, society as a whole, or to the Davidians from continuing this standoff and that the possibility of a peaceful resolution continued to exist."

The 1995 hearings did not bring closure to the case of the Waco Siege and in many ways seemed to have exacerbated the situation and raised more questions, which in turn gave fuel to more conspiracy theories. In July of 2000, around the same time that the Supreme Court reduced the sentences of the incarcerated Branch Davidians, and when many were being released from prison, former U.S. Senator John Danforth of Missouri led another congressional hearing of the Waco Siege.

Although Danforth was a Republican, he was appointed by Janet Reno as "Special Council" to oversee the hearings. Not as extensive as the 1995 hearings, the 2000 hearings essentially absolved the federal government of responsibility for the deaths of the Branch Davidians during the siege.

But not everyone was happy with the government's assessment of the Waco Siege.

The Rise of the Militia Movement

Among the conspiracy theorists that received ample fodder for their ideas due to the Waco Siege some of the more radical ones came from the militia movement. The genesis of the militia movement can be traced to the patriot movement of the 1960s, the Posse Comitatus movement of the 1970s, and the survivalist craze of the 1980s. Each of these played a considerable role in its formation, but the Waco Siege seemed to be the event that saw them coalesce into a viable movement.

The patriot movement began in the 1950s as a militant offshoot of the right wing John Birch Society that believed an armed conflict with the Soviet Union, the U.S. federal government, or both, was imminent. The patriots opposed the Civil Rights movement, as they believed it was a Communist plot, but eschewed protests and political lobbying in favor of military training. The patriots also believed in several conspiracy theories.

As the United States moved into the 1970s many members of the patriot movement joined a growing subset known as the Posse Comitatus (Latin for "force of the county") movement.

The Posse Comitatus movement held many of the same political beliefs and conspiracy theories of the patriot movement of the 1970s, but adopted a more racialist and anti-Semitic tone, as they attributed the perpetrators of many of the conspiracies they believed in to "Zionists." The Posse Comitatus was a movement, not a unified group, so beliefs and practices ranged from locations, but all followers practiced firearms training to the point that some groups resembled paramilitary organizations. Posse Comitatus members also practiced survivalism because they believed either the United States government would collapse or the country would be invaded by the Soviet Union.

During the 1980s, as U.S. president Reagan's rhetoric towards the Soviet Union became more incendiary, the threat of World War III once more became a possibility in many Americans' minds. Many Americans began to stockpile weapons and food in the hope that if such a war were to occur, they could somehow survive. Most of the adherents of this philosophy came from the right wing of the political spectrum, but a number of leftists also practiced and continue to practice survivalism. By the early 1990s these various strains of thoughts combined to produce the militia movement.

The primary focus of the militia movement was the Second Amendment, which the followers believed entitled Americans the right not only to bear arms, but also to form private paramilitary organizations known as militias. As a historical precedent, militia leaders pointed to the militias of the American Revolution, which were privately formed paramilitary groups that fought the British occupation. Like the Posse Comitatus movement before them, the militia movement was decentralized and comprised of several different organizations across the country. Unlike the Posse Comitatus movement, the militia for the most part eschewed racialist and anti-Semitic ideas, but were big proponents of conspiracy theories.

The Waco Siege appeared tailor made for the militia movement.

In the days, weeks, and months following the Waco Siege, groups such as the Michigan Militia and the Militia of Montana began to become more visible as their leaders gave numerous interviews to various media outlets and they were often the subject of investigative reports. Militia leaders claimed that the Waco Siege was part of a much broader government conspiracy meant to disarm the citizenry in order to enact marshal law.

In the end, most militia members did not go beyond rhetoric and by the late 1990s the movement had lost most of its inertia. The movement was further hurt by the events of April 19, 1995.

On the second anniversary of the FBI's raid on Mount Carmel, a large truck bomb was detonated outside the Alfred P. Murrah Federal building in Oklahoma City, Oklahoma. The bombing left 168 people dead and nearly 700 injured and was, up until September 11, 2001, the worst terrorist attack in United States history. The primary culprit of the act was Tim McVeigh, who was one of the many supporters of the Branch Davidians present at the media camp outside Mount Carmel. Although not a member of any militia group, McVeigh related in interviews conducted after his conviction for the bombing that the act was done in retaliation for the government's role in the Waco Siege, among other perceived acts of government oppression. McVeigh was convicted of the bombing in 1997 and sentenced to death, which was carried out in 2001. Some scholars have argued that McVeigh's bombing was the death knell of the militia movement as it led to a series of raids and arrests by the government and forced the "hobbyists" to give up the movement, but also sent the more radical members underground where they still exist today.

Some Last Notes on Those Involved with the Waco Siege

The Waco Siege truly touched the lives of many people involved in a number of different ways. Most of the law enforcement officers involved went on with their careers and several have since retired. The questionable conduct and character of Judge Walter Smith, which was called into question when he presided over both the Branch Davidians' criminal and civil trials, has recently been confirmed in many people's eyes.

On December 3, 2015 Smith was suspended from office for a year due to a report of sexual assault by a female courthouse employee stemming an incident that allegedly took place in 1998.

Mark England and Darlene McCormick, the writers of the "Sinful Messiah" series for the *Waco Tribune,* were both given the Managing Editor's Award for their "public service" by the Associated Press in September, 1933.

The Branch Davidian survivors have had a more difficult time picking up the pieces.

All of the foreign members who were convicted of crimes related to the Waco Siege were deported back to their countries of origin after they were released from prison and all have had trouble to varying degrees adjusting to life after prison. Some have written memoirs and given public lectures on their experiences, but nearly all have clung to their strict SDA beliefs.

The child survivors of the Waco Siege present an interesting story that is still unfolding. Some of the children have gone on to college, while others have started families and at least one went into law enforcement as a career. Most of the children have been fairly private about their experiences, but their experiences from those fifty one days, when and if any decide to go public, will offer a new perspective on the American tragedy.

Conclusion

In terms of recent decades, the Waco Siege is probably the worst disaster in American history. Yes, Waco was a tragedy because so many lives were lost, especially those of the innocent children, but what makes it so difficult for many to grasp is that it could have been avoided.

At numerous steps the federal government could have stepped back and let the situation "cool down." The ATF could have arrested David Koresh off the grounds of Mount Carmel without doing a "dynamic entry" and the FBI could have waited longer instead of raiding the complex on April 19: after all the Branch Davidians only had a finite food supply. The use of CS inside Mount Carmel was at best a bad decision and at worst criminally negligent. With that said, Koresh and the Branch Davidians made their fair share of mistakes during the siege.

It is true that Koresh allowed his followers to leave Mount Carmel during the siege and many in fact did, but a good leader leads by example. If Koresh would have surrendered to the FBI while Gary Noesner was still the lead negotiator, then the bloodshed of April 19 would most likely never have happened.

But Koresh was not the only Branch Davidian to blame.

Although Koresh may have been a charismatic leader with great influence over his followers, they were still adults with free will and explicit rights under the Constitution in which they claimed to believe. The adults who stayed after the February 28 raid do so under their own volition and no matter what Koresh or the government said, in the end they could have left at any time.

Finally, the government, from President Bill Clinton down to ground level federal agents, can only blame themselves for allowing the plethora of conspiracy theories to proliferate in the years since the Waco Siege. By not being more forthcoming initially, the average American has since viewed the congressional hearings of 1995 and 2000 as little more than kangaroo courts, which has given more credence to the conspiracy theorists. More government transparency in the weeks after the siege may have prevented this attitude from taking hold.

Ultimately, when people ask if the tragedy of the Waco Siege could have been prevented the answer is not so simple. Yes, both sides made numerous mistakes along the way that aggravated the situation, but the essence of the situation – a breakaway sect in possession of an extremely large amount of guns – is something that is protected by the United States Constitution for the most part. Yes, there are limits to both the First and Second Amendments, but determining those limits can be costly as evidenced by the Waco Siege.

A Note From The Author

Hello, this is Jack Rosewood. Thank you for reading The Waco Siege: An American Tragedy. I hope you enjoyed the read of this historical event. If you did, I'd appreciate if you would take a few moments to post a review on Amazon.

Best Regards
Jack Rosewood

Bibliography

Docherty, Jayne Seminare. "Why Waco Has Not Gone Away: Critical Incidents and Cultural Trauma." *Novo Religio: The Journal of Alternative and Emergent Religions* 5 (2001): 186-202.

Kerkstetter, Todd. "'That's Just the American Way': The Branch Davidian Tragedy and Western Religious History." *Western Historical Quarterly* 35 (2004): 453-471.

Reavis, Dick J. *The Ashes of Waco: An Investigation*. Syracuse, New York: Syracuse University Press, 1998.

Wessinger, Catherine. "Deaths in the Fire at the Branch Davidians' Mount Carmel: Who Bears Responsibility?" *Novo Religio: The Journal of Alternative and Emergent Religions* 13 (2009): 25-60.

Wright, Stuart A. "A Decade after Waco: Reassessing Crisis Negotiations at Mount Carmel in Light of New Government Disclosures." *Novo Religio: The Journal of Alternative and Emergent Religions* 7 (2003): 101-110.

Printed in Great Britain
by Amazon